# Salaah Is a Blessing, *Not* a Burden

## Ten Blessings of Prayer We Often Overlook

### NEW EDITION

*by* Umm Zakiyyah

**Salaah Is a Blessing, Not a Burden: Ten Blessings of Prayer We Often Overlook (New Edition)**
by Umm Zakiyyah



Order information at **uzauthor.com**

UZ Soul Care info at **uzuniversity.com** and **uzhearthub.com**

Arabic script of Qur'an from corpus.quran.com. English excerpts from the Qur'an are taken from Saheeh International, Darussalam, and Yusuf Ali translations of meanings.

Cover photo © by Ali Arapoglu from Pexels

Published by Al-Walaa Publications
Gwynn Oak, Maryland  USA

# Table of Contents

# Author's Note

This book, along with its corresponding course, initially began as a compilation of the notes and reflections from a live webinar I hosted entitled "Salaah, a Blessing, Not a Burden," held on the 8th of Dhul-Hijjah 1441, corresponding to July 29th, 2020. Thus, the project was initially intended as a supplement to the course and coursebook entitled *Come Back To Allah, Dear Soul* via uzhearthub.com. However, as I began to compile the notes, a new course and book emerged.

At the heart of this book and corresponding course is the spiritual message that mirrors the one shared in the original Salaah course and book: *There is no salvation or spiritual health without the Salaah.*

Salaah is the second pillar of Islam after the *shahaadah*, the formal testimony of faith wherein a person bears witness that nothing has the right to be worshipped except Allah alone and that Prophet Muhammad ﷺ is His last and final prophet and messenger. Specifically, Salaah refers to the five foundational prayers of the Muslim—*Fajr, Dhuhr, 'Asr, Maghrib,* and *Ishaa*—as well as any voluntary formal prayer such as *Witr, Qiyaam al-Layl,* or any of the other Sunnah prayers that complement the obligatory Salaah.

This book discusses the pivotal role that Salaah holds in the Muslim's spiritual life, as well as its numerous blessings. I give a glimpse into these innumerable blessings here. This book further serves as a reminder that the central spiritual role of the five foundational prayers in our *deen*—our spiritual way of life—is second to only *Tawheed* (the Oneness of Allah) itself, as the five pillars of our faith demonstrate quite clearly. Therefore, the role that Salaah holds for both the salvation of our souls in the Hereafter and our spiritual health in this world cannot and should not be trivialized.

In this book, I share ten blessings that we often overlook when we fully embrace Salaah as the spiritual foundation of our *emaan*—the single most significant manifestation of true faith in the believer's heart. In the second part of this book, I also include "Soul Reflections" journal prompts after each blessing mentioned. This is so that you as the reader can reflect on the unique significance of Salaah to you personally for each topic covered.

I pray that you find in this compilation both inspiration and benefit during your brief sojourn in this world.

*May Allah make the Salaah a source of joy and tranquility for you until you meet Him, and may He write you down amongst His most beloved and sincere companions of Salaah and Qur'an in this world and in the Hereafter.*

Your sister in faith,

August 26th, 2024
22nd of Safar, 1446 AH

"O dear soul who rushes through Prayer,
Is there somewhere you absolutely must go…
Other than Jannah?"
—from the journal of Umm Zakiyyah

# Part One
## *Why Salaah Feels Burdensome*

# 1

## *Showing Up Empty*

When I was struggling to hold on to my *emaan*, I used to dread when it was time to pray. Just mustering the strength to perform *wudhoo'* and stand for Salaah felt so overwhelming. There were moments that I would even crawl to the Salaah because I felt so depressed and unmotivated to pray. So, whenever I found myself standing (or sitting) for prayer, my heart wasn't really in it, and deep inside, I felt spiritually empty.

As I recited *Al-Faatihah* (the first *soorah* of the Qur'an) and fulfilled the other requirements of Salaah, I was just going through the motions. Nevertheless, though I didn't really want to, I kept showing up for Salaah day after day. I told myself that an empty, ritualistic prayer was better than no prayer at all. And based on what I've known for quite some time regarding the weightiness of Salaah in the Muslim's life, I was right.

However, at the time, reminding myself of the religious significance of Salaah did little to nourish my spiritual wounds. More significantly, it did little to make me feel connected to my Rabb in any meaningful way. Yet it was this spiritual connection that my heart ached for during this difficult time. But instead, while offering my half-hearted prayers, I felt like Salaah was just a weighty burden that I had to fulfill because I wanted to be counted as a Muslim.

It was during this time of emotional pain and spiritual emptiness that I wrote a personal note in my journal that continues to motivate and inspire me till today:

*Struggling in your emaan? Do you feel dead inside when you pray, make du'aa, or read Qur'an?*

*Remember this: It's okay to show up empty.*

*Just be sure to show up.*

*And your Lord will fill your heart with the spiritual fuel it needs, eventually.*

*But you have to show up.*

*Show up to prayer.*

*Show up to du'aa.*

*Show up to Qur'an.*

*Just the act of showing up is a powerful act of faith.*

*Allah will take care of the rest.*

The truth is, no matter how empty or overwhelmed we feel at times, Salaah is an immense mercy and blessing from Allah. However, for the struggling believer, acknowledging this spiritual reality does little to lighten the burden of Salaah on the heart. This is why, for so many of us, Salaah continues to feel burdensome even when we mentally understand its merciful significance in our faith.

But why?

# 2

## *Are You Nourishing Your Spiritual Veins?*

When seeking the answer to why Salaah can feel so burdensome even with knowledge of its merciful significance, here's something we can reflect on: After the *shahaadah* itself, Salaah is the primary source of spiritual life for the believer. This source of life is comparable to how after oxygen in the lungs, water is the primary source of physical life for the human being. Therefore, if we are deprived of any crucial aspects of the Salaah within our hearts, then it is like we are being deprived of the minimal amount of water we need in our bodies to avoid physical dehydration—and in the case of our hearts, we are becoming spiritually dehydrated.

In other words, whenever Salaah begins to feel overwhelming and burdensome for us, then our spiritual veins are "thirsty" and in need of vital nourishment to strengthen the heart. And we get this nourishment from striving to connect to our Rabb each day—even when we feel unmotivated—through continuing to show up for Salaah despite feeling spiritually empty.

During this time of emotional overwhelm and spiritual emptiness, we might begin to ask ourselves, "What's the point?" This is a question that my struggling heart battled during some of my lowest points. And the truth is, the struggle is real, so there really isn't any one answer that will "magically" heal our hearts and make us suddenly feel motivated to pray. Moreover, even when our mind understands the "theoretical" reasons why we pray, our heart is not always open, ready, or strong enough to accept it.

Nevertheless, I'll share something that I reminded myself and my sisters and brothers in faith some time ago, and I pray the reminder benefits each of us on our spiritual journeys: *So many of us abandon our worship—our spiritual fuel—when we feel empty. But would you abandon going to the fuel (petrol) station if your car was on "E"? Emptiness is a sign that you need that fuel most.*

# 3
## *Spiritual Dehydration*

If you ask anyone about the importance of hydrating the body with water or having access to clean water each day, they would almost certainly affirm that fresh, unpolluted water is an absolute necessity. They would also almost certainly affirm that without this water hydrating your veins each day, you would die. Furthermore, many would affirm that water is so vital to our bodies that it is more essential than food, because our bodies need much more water than food.

Nevertheless, despite our widespread knowledge about the necessity of water, it is not uncommon for us to neglect drinking the minimum amount of water we need for optimal physical health. Moreover, so many of us consume much more food than water, and we continuously drink beverages that are bad for our health, even as we have fresh drinking water all around us.  It is indeed ironic that this neglect of our health is most common in regions of the world where we have access to clean water every single day.

## Dehydration of the Body

When our bodies do not intake as much water as we need, we suffer from dehydration, which if left untreated, can lead to death. Symptoms of dehydration include dizziness, body weakness, muscle cramps, headaches, and poor urine output. The last symptom is a sign that our body is not healthily cleansing itself and expelling harmful toxins. In combination, all of these symptoms are serious red flags that the life of our physical body is in danger.

At the moment of dehydration, it is not uncommon for a person to feel unmotivated to do the things they would normally do throughout the day, even important tasks that include self-care and caring for vulnerable loved ones who depend on them.

When we are in a state of dehydration, it can become difficult to function, to think clearly, or to even muster the energy to properly hydrate the body and do what it needs to survive. Sometimes we end up in a clinic or hospital with IV (intravenous) fluids being forced into our veins as a desperate attempt to save our life.

During moments of dehydration, we might mentally know what we need to do for self-care and hydration. However, due to the harm that the dehydration has caused us, we quite likely do not have the physical or mental energy to take care of ourselves properly. Consequently, self-care and even proper hydration can feel burdensome.

This feeling of overwhelm in no way indicates that we actually view water itself as an inherent burden to our bodies and lives. It just means that our dehydration has sapped so much of our physical and mental energy that we need a bit of encouragement, beneficial reminders, physical assistance with hydration and self-care, or even medical intervention until we have regained our physical and mental strength.

## Spiritual Dehydration

Similarly, when begin to feel that the Salaah is a burden, we are undergoing a form of spiritual dehydration that affects our hearts and souls similar to how physical dehydration affects our bodies and physical strength. In this state, we can know that the Salaah—like water with our physical health—

will cleanse spiritually damaging toxins from our hearts and souls, but we might lack the health and vigor to do what's necessary to properly hydrate our spiritual veins.

Meanwhile, like water in our physical nourishment, Salaah itself remains a tremendous blessing and an essential form of spiritual nourishment or "hydration" to the soul. Unfortunately, however, when we are spiritually dehydrated, our hearts and minds begin to lose the spiritual strength to consciously experience Salaah as the immeasurable mercy and blessing that it is.

# 4

## *Help Them Suffer Dehydration?*

In the course *Come Back To Allah, Dear Soul,* I discuss a concept that I call *compassionate misguidance.* This term refers to any damaging spiritual advice that is intended to show compassion and encouragement to those who are struggling with the foundational prayers, but is in reality rooted in concepts that harm our souls and exacerbate our "spiritual dehydration," despite the (likely) good intentions of the advisor.

One of the most spiritually harmful examples of compassionate misguidance is telling a person that it's okay if they feel too weak, too depressed, or too lazy to pray; and that they can just wait until they feel spiritually strong or mentally motivated before resuming the Salaah. Or they tell them that it's okay to neglect prayers on a regular basis, or to pray only one pray a day, if that's all they feel motivated to do.

In other words, in the name of compassion and empathy, these "compassionate advisors" encourage a soul already suffering from spiritual dehydration to dehydrate their souls even more. In this, they are pushing an already dying, suffering soul to exacerbate their condition by depriving themselves of the single most crucial source of life that will rejuvenate them and restore their spiritual health.

Figuratively speaking, these compassionate advisors do this because they believe that advising a person in the throes of dehydration to patiently lift their head to take a sip of water or to patiently withstand the discomfort of an IV needle being placed in their arm to save their life, is being unkind and judgmental, or "too strict" and extreme.

They feel that the "judgmental person" putting water to someone's lips or an IV in their veins to save them doesn't understand what the dehydrated person is going through. In this way, these "compassionate advisors" accuse the very one who is saving this person's life of being too ignorant, insensitive, or arrogant to just leave the dehydrated person alone. Thus, in the minds of these compassionate advisors, what is healthiest and most helpful for the dehydrated person is to just leave them alone and watch them die.

They claim that this passive, "compassionate" approach is most necessary if the energy required to hydrate the person—or if the instructions that encourage them to hydrate themselves—inspires even the slightly discomfort or pain. As a result, they intentionally abandon this person in their most desperate time of need.

These advisors defend themselves by claiming that spiritual death is exponentially better than the dying person *ever* feeling any irritation, discomfort, or pain in the process of someone trying to save their life.

## They Both Need Help

Undoubtedly, those who assign themselves to the role of compassionate supporter to someone suffering spiritual dehydration and then proceed to merely watch them die— and do nothing except actively stop those who are trying to save their life—are themselves suffering from a spiritual ailment that needs treatment. This spiritual ailment might be sincere, misguided ignorance; or it could be a spiritual disease of the heart wherein they (consciously or unconsciously) dislike what Allah loves and loves what He dislikes.

Either way, intervention is needed to help them understand that they are harming themselves and others. The intervention that "compassionate advisors" need is just as crucial as the intervention that the spiritually dehydrated person needs, as both are spiritually unwell, and critically so. In fact, the person calling to compassionate misguidance is suffering a more serious spiritual ailment than mere dehydration, as their spiritual health issue has reached such a toxic level that their hearts and minds are "nourished" by actively seeking others' spiritual dehydration and, thus, their ultimate spiritual death.

In this way, the misguided compassionate advisor is like a person suffering addiction to drugs or alcohol who feels most at ease not only when harming their own bodies with these destructive toxins, but also when inviting friends and loved ones to join in. In this, they are like someone who genuinely views sober, healthy people as missing out on the "joys of life," so they make it their mission to make sure everyone around them has a "happy and fun" life.

In other words, their entire philosophy of life is a damaging form of hedonism, which is the ideology that pleasure or happiness is the sole purpose of life. And since drugs and alcohol are (in their minds) the chief sources of pleasure and happiness in life, these addicts see it as their "duty" to ensure that everyone they come in contact with "enjoys" drugs and alcohol, too.

In the spiritual realm, compassionate advisors are hedonists with regards to spirituality just as these "social addicts" are hedonists with regards to drugs and alcohol. In their life of spiritual hedonism, they genuinely imagine that the entire purpose of spirituality is to feel pleasure and happiness every moment of your life—even if the path you take to achieve it can almost certainly ensure your death.

Figuratively speaking, the spiritual hedonist who identifies as Muslim genuinely believes that a dying person avoiding the physical discomfort of lifting his (or her) head or withstanding the poke of a needle while he is already in pain and discomfort, is more crucial than assisting him in doing what is necessary to save his life.

So, naturally, just as the addicts who see their habitual drug or alcohol use as a good thing would never support drug intervention programs or groups like AA (alcoholics anonymous), spiritual hedonists who identify as Muslim would never support spiritual interventions aimed at saving a Muslim's spiritual life, at least not unless they can be absolutely sure that every aspect of this intervention will make the person "happy." Yet their hedonistic ideology just points to their own urgent need for spiritual intervention themselves.

# 5

## *Getting Spiritually Hydrated*

It is undeniable that the only way to address physical dehydration is to hydrate the body with water so that the hydration reaches the veins of the body as soon as possible. Similarly, the only way to address spiritual dehydration is to hydrate the soul with Salaah so that the hydration reaches the spiritual "veins" of the heart as soon as possible. In both cases of dehydration, whether physical or spiritual, how a person mentally or emotionally *feels* about hydrating their body or soul is irrelevant to the urgency of them actually getting hydrated.

At the moment of dehydration, the most urgent matter is to rehydrate oneself and then commit to a daily regimen of hydration to prevent recurrent dehydration in the future. Depending on the level of mental or emotional struggles the person has with daily hydration, this daily commitment to one's health and wellness, whether physical or spiritual, can feel tremendously overwhelming and burdensome. Nevertheless, committing to the daily regimen of hydration—physically and spiritually—is an absolute necessity, as it is literally "life or death" for your body and soul.

While spiritual hydration is an absolute necessity irrespective of how we feel about that hydration, this does not mean we should ignore our feelings completely. It just means that these feelings should not prevent us from continuing to spiritually hydrate ourselves.

Furthermore, though Salaah is the most essential source of spiritual hydration after *Tawheed* itself, this does not mean that praying Salaah should be our *only* means of addressing our spiritual dehydration. Undoubtedly, underlying issues like mental health conditions, unresolved emotional trauma, and unhealed spiritual wounding directly affect our spiritual health and thus can disrupt our ability to feel fully hydrated through the Salaah.

For this reason, when Salaah feels continuously burdensome, it is crucial that we supplement our worship with proper mental healthcare, emotional healing, and seeking to understand and address our underlying spiritual wounding. What this particular aspect of spiritual hydration will look like will vary from person to person, but for each of us, this personalized self-care is essential to our soul-care.

## Allah Knows What You're Going Through

In the Qur'an, our Merciful Creator lets us know that He knows our struggles, and He acknowledges how emotionally heavy and burdensome they sometimes feel. In His immeasurable knowledge and wisdom, He also gives us the formula for seeking help in getting the holistic rehydration that our hearts and souls need, despite how overwhelming this lifestyle of spiritual health and emotional wellness can feel at times.

He says,

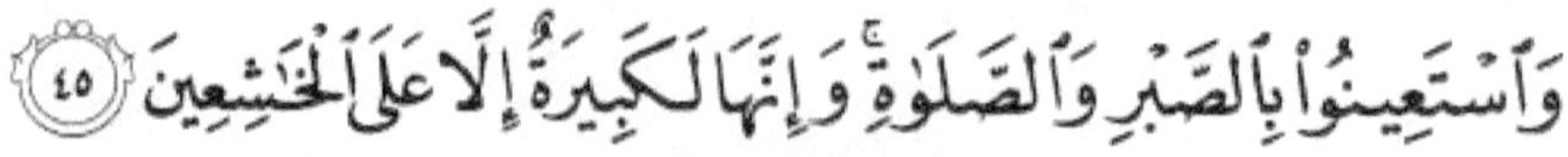

This *ayah* has been translated to mean,

**"And seek help in *Sabr* (patiently persevering upon what nourishes the soul and betters one's life) and the**

**Salaah, and truly it is extremely heavy and hard except for the *Khaashi'oon* (the humbly submissive)"**
*(Al-Baqarah*, 2:45).

So often the term *sabr* is translated as simply *patience*. However, *sabr* actually refers to a lifestyle of soul care and self-care, whether one is enjoying times of ease and happiness or suffering times of difficulty and distress. Inherent in the definition of *sabr* is persevering upon this lifestyle of spiritual, personal, and emotional wellness even when it is difficult, as discussed in the definition below.

## Sabr As Spiritual Hydration

Specifically, *sabr* means two things: (1) patiently persevering upon what nourishes the soul and betters our life, even when we feel emotionally weak and overwhelmed (or mentally burdened and exhausted); and (2) patiently persevering upon withholding ourselves from doing anything that harms our soul or practical life, even when we feel inclined to or tempted toward a path of self-harm, whether spiritually, personally, or emotionally.

Additionally, with respect to both of these aspects of the definition, *sabr* means seeking the proper help from our Creator while also utilizing the merciful resources He's given us through His creation that support us on the path to optimal spiritual health, emotional wellness, and personal life betterment.

Also inherent in the definition of *sabr* is to continuously seek repentance when (not *if*) we sin or fall short in our efforts, and to subsequently return to a lifestyle of soul nourishment and personal improvement no matter how many times we have to get back up when we fall and no matter how many times we have to "start over" when we deviate from the right path.

As it relates to Salaah in particular, *sabr* means committing to a daily lifestyle of giving the heart and soul at least the bare minimum hydration they need for spiritual survival. As aforementioned, spiritually speaking, after *Tawheed* itself, the bare minimum hydration that the soul needs is patiently nourishing the heart with the five foundational prayers, no matter how emotionally or mentally burdensome this spiritual rehydration feels.

# 6

## *Salaah As Tawheed of the Limbs*

We know that the five foundational prayers reflect the bare minimum spiritual hydration that our souls need because this is what we are taught in the *Kitaab* (the Book of Allah) and the *Hikmah* (the divinely inspired prophetic teachings). The divine evidences that establish the absolute spiritual necessity of Salaah are too numerous for this context. However, for the sake of clarity, I will mention one evidence from the *Kitaab* and one evidence from the *Hikmah*.

In the Surah (divine chapter) of Qur'an entitled *Al-Muddaththir*, Allah gives us a glimpse of what will happen in the Hereafter with regards to the believers and disbelievers. In one set of *ayaat*, He shares with us a conversation between the people of Paradise and the people of Hellfire. When the people of Hellfire are asked what caused them to enter it, the very first reason they mention is that they were not of those who prayed. Allah says,

These *ayaat* have been translated to mean:

**"Every soul, for what it has earned, will be retained. Except the companions of the right, [who will be] in gardens, questioning each other, about the criminals, [and asking them], 'What put you into *Saqar* (Hellfire)?' They will say, 'We were not of those who prayed...'"**
(*Al-Muddaththir*, 74:38-42).

In further emphasizing Salaah as a bare minimum necessity for the soul's spiritual survival, Prophet Muhammad (peace and blessings be upon him) said, "What is between a person and committing *shirk* (associating partners with Allah) and *kufr* (disbelief) is abandoning the Salaah" (Sahih Muslim).

As I discuss in the Salaah coursebook and course videos for *Come Back To Allah, Dear Soul*: While the *shahaadah* is *Tawheed* of the heart and tongue, Salaah is the most foundational manifestation of the *Tawheed* of the limbs.

## Tawheed in Our Hearts and Lives

In Islam, the term *Tawheed* refers to authentic monotheism as reflected in the Oneness of Allah. When *Tawheed* enters the heart, spiritually speaking, it is manifested in three comprehensive ways:

(1) sincere belief in Allah alone as our Rabb (Guardian Lord) who is the Creator, Owner, and Manager of all that exists, whether seen or unseen.

(2) singling out Allah alone in our worship and ultimate obedience; having in our hearts sincere love, hope, and fear of Allah in a way that transcends how we experience these same feelings with respect to any of His creation; and trusting in the guidance and teachings of Allah over all other ideologies and systems of guidance such that our hearts are fully content with Allah as the ultimate authority in our spiritual, personal, and community life.

(3) believing in the divine Oneness and Uniqueness of all of Allah's Names and Attributes while assigning none of His Names or Attributes to any of His creation (and while assigning none of His creation's attributes to Him); affirming everything that Allah says about Himself without anthropomorphic assumptions that inspire figurative interpretations of divine attributes that are incomprehensible to the fallible human mind; and never allowing the mind or heart to deny, change, or reinterpret the apparent meaning what Allah says about Himself, even when that apparent meaning isn't apparent to us.

As it relates to its practical manifestation in the believer's life, every aspect of *Tawheed* discussed above can be summarized into three categories: belief, speech, and action. Alternatively, its manifestation can be explained through two simple categories: internal manifestation of *Tawheed* and external manifestation of *Tawheed*.

The most basic and essential internal manifestation of *Tawheed* is *emaan* (sincere faith) itself, which is reflected in a heart that is free from any *shirk* or *kufr*. After reciting the *shahaadah* itself, the most basic and essential external manifestation of *Tawheed* is establishing the Salaah, the five foundational prayers, every day without fail until we are lowered beneath the ground.

In this way, after sincere belief in the Oneness of Allah, Salaah is the most essential spiritual hydration for the soul and thereby preserves *Tawheed* in the believer's heart.

If we go back to the analogy of physical life and health, we can understand the *shahaadah* as the oxygen in our lungs and establishing the Salaah as the water in our veins. If you deprive the body or soul of either source of life, death is inevitable. That is, unless you restore air to the lungs and water to the veins—i.e. *emaan* to the heart and prayer to the limbs—before the soul leaves the body.

# 7

## *Too Far To Walk?*

Before discussing the numerous benefits of the Salaah, one final reflection we can consider in seeking to understand what is happening when Salaah feels burdensome (and we thus feel unmotivated to pray) is this hypothetical scenario:

Imagine you've lost all your wealth and your home, and you and your family are now living on the streets. Each day, you live in agony, having no idea where your next meal will come from, where you will sleep at night, or how you and your family will be safe from the heat or cold—or from the vicious criminals that roam the streets each night.

Then one day, someone walks up to you and tells you that an anonymous person has given you and your family one million dollars, and all you have to do is go to the nearest bank and pick it up. They tell you that you can use the money to purchase any comfortable, safe home that you like and to buy meals for yourself and your family each day. They also tell you that not only do you *not* have to pay this person back, but also that if you continue to use the money to support yourself and your family, this person will continue to deposit money into your account for as long as you live.

Imagine how ecstatic, relieved, and grateful you would feel at that moment.

But now imagine that after the initial moment of excitement passes, you begin to mentally calculate how to get to the nearest bank, which is three blocks away. Concerned, you realize that you don't have a car, so you have no choice but to walk there to pick up the generous donation.

Logically speaking, this isn't an extremely long walk, and you know this. But still, you think of how exhausted you already feel from living on the streets and going hungry each day. You think of how mentally spent you feel at just the thought of facing another day. You then recall how your legs ache each day due to the excessive walking you already do just to survive.

Now you begin to feel overwhelmed and stressed about picking up the check because, quite frankly, you just don't feel like going through the mental, emotional, and physical discomfort that the walk requires from you. So you begin to complain to your family about having to walk "all the way" to the bank to pick up that check. You openly ask why this so-called "generous donor" decided to put the check "in some faraway bank" and not directly in your hands. "If they were *truly* generous," you say, "I wouldn't even have to *go* anywhere to pick it up in the first place. They would be compassionate enough to just bring it to me. Can't they see all the stress I'm under?"

Then finally you say to yourself, *I'm not going to pick up that check because walking three blocks is just too far for me, given how exhausted and overwhelmed I already feel.*

So, in that moment, you are willing to continue living in poverty and desperation, to continue suffering potential starvation and dehydration, and to continue subjecting yourself and your family to fear, crime, and danger. All because in your mental and emotional overwhelm, you feel that patiently withstanding the physical and mental discomfort of walking the three blocks—which would literally solve *all* of your immediate problems—simply is not worth the stress.

Does this mindset make any sense to you? If your answer is no—as I'm sure it most certainly would be—then consider this reality: It makes *more* sense to think this way than to view Salaah as a burden.

In other words, it is more sensible—and less harmful, in fact—to refuse to pick up that check due to your personal struggles than to refuse to pray Salaah due to feeling burdened and overwhelmed. Why?

Let's look at just a small portion of the numerous mercies and blessings of Salaah, as expounded in the next section. Then *bi'idhnillaah*, this glimpse into the immeasurable *rahmah* of formal prayer will help us understand how Salaah is exponentially more valuable and essential to our life than any physical comfort, success, or wealth in this world.

# Part Two
## *Mercies and Blessings of Salaah*

# Blessing 1
## *Salaah Reflects the Essential Mercy of Our Deen*

In the Qur'an, Allah teaches us that He has perfected our religion for us, has completed His favor upon us, and has chosen for us Islam as our *deen*, our spiritual way of life. In this excerpt of a longer *ayah*, Allah says what has been translated to mean, **"This day, I have perfected your religion for you, completed My Favor upon you, and have chosen for you Islam as your *deen*"** (*Al-Maa'idah*, 5:3).

In explaining the foundations of this spiritual favor from our Rabb (our Merciful Creator), Prophet Muhammad (peace and blessings be upon him) said, "Islam is built on five [pillars]: testifying that nothing has the right to be worshipped except Allah alone and that Muhammad is the Messenger of Allah; establishing the Salaah; paying the *zakat* (obligatory charity); making Hajj to the House (i.e. the *Ka'bah* in Makkah); and fasting in Ramadan" (Bukhari and Muslim).

Regarding the essence of this *deen*, Allah explains to Prophet Muhammad the purpose of his prophetic mission, in which he was sent as the last prophet and messenger to humankind until the Day of Judgment. Allah says,

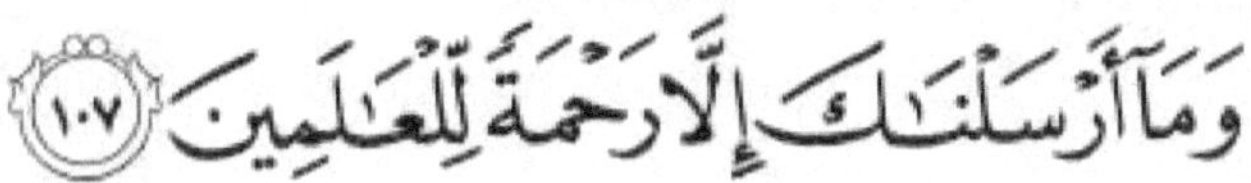

This *ayah* has been translated to mean, **"And We have not sent you, [O Muhammad], except as a mercy to the worlds"** (*Al-Anbiyaa*, 21:107).

From this *ayah*, along with numerous other divine evidences from the *Kitaab* and *Hikmah*, we learn that the essence of *rahmah* (i.e. divine mercy and compassion) is at the heart of our *deen*. Therefore, every pillar of Islam is a direct reflection of this spiritual and practical *rahmah*, which has been gifted to us by our Merciful Rabb.

In other words, as it pertains to Salaah in particular, since the guidance that the Prophet ﷺ brought from Allah is at its root a mission of mercy to all of creation, then the second pillar of this spiritual guidance must be a direct reflection of that *rahmah*—that divine mercy. In the following chapters, *bi'idhnillaah*, these numerous blessings will be enumerated, thereby further illustrating the immeasurable mercy that we have in the Salaah.

## Soul Reflections

*As it relates to the blessing of Salaah that you just read about, write freely from your heart. Or respond to this journal prompt: When you reflect on the ayah about Prophet Muhammad (peace and blessings be upon him) being sent as a mercy to all the worlds, think about the different "worlds" around you (i.e. emotional, spiritual, personal, financial, nature, etc.). What are some ways that the spiritual way of life found in the Qur'an and prophetic teachings have brought mercy and blessings to you, to your environment, or to someone you know (even if they are not Muslim)?*

# Blessing 2
## *Salaah Is Success*

In my course *Come Back To Allah, Dear Soul,* I share a reflection from my journal in which I recall a conversation I had with my mother:

"How did you do it?" I asked my Mom one day. "Wasn't it hard raising all of us?" There was awe and exhaustion in my tone—awe because my mother had birthed and raised fifteen children. Yet she maintained a sense of peaceful presence that I couldn't even fathom amidst my own exhaustion in raising just one.

"It was hard," she admitted, a reflective honesty in her tone. "And there were days I had no idea how you all would turn out. But whenever I'd get really worried or stressed, Allah would make something happen, like I would be calling your name and you wouldn't answer. Then I'd get really frustrated and come to your room to get you. But when I opened the door, I'd find you in *sajdah* (prostrating in prayer to Allah). Then my heart would calm, and I'd say to myself, *They're going to be all right.*"

What was it that gave my mother's heart this calm reassurance, this tranquil certainty? It was the knowledge that no significant harm could come to the life or soul of anyone for whom Salaah is an integral part of their life and a foundational part of their day.

Naturally, this doesn't mean that a person who establishes the Salaah will face no difficulty in life. It just means that a person whose daily life is built around the five foundational prayers possesses the "master key" to turning every trial into a spiritual purification for the soul and a tremendous blessing for their life. This is because Salaah is not only the path to worldly and spiritual success, Salaah is also success itself.

## Come To Prayer, Come To Success

The merciful reality that Salaah equals success is precisely what we are being told every day five times a day when we are called to prayer. In the *adhaan* (the official call to prayer), the muezzin calls out what can be translated to mean, "Come to Salaah. Come to success."

When Allah in His infinite knowledge and wisdom, inspired Prophet Muhammad ﷺ to appoint the famous companion Bilal ibn Rabah (may Allah be pleased with him) to use his strong, moving voice to call out these words at the time of every foundational prayer, Al-Hakeem (the All-Wise) was not only establishing the merciful Sunnah of the *adhaan*, He was also sending the ummah of Muhammad a message that would resonate in their hearts until the end of time: Salaah is success itself.

In the Qur'an, Allah says,

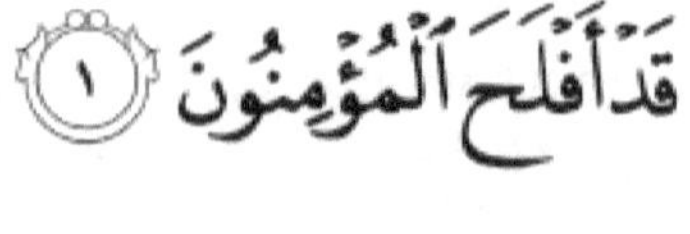

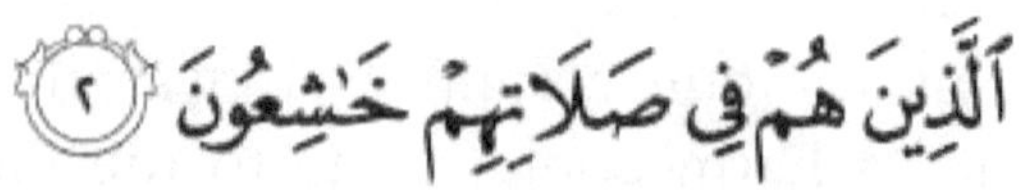

These two *ayaat* have been translated to mean, **"Successful indeed are the believers. Those who offer their Salaah with humility, sincerity, and full submissiveness"** (*Al-Mu'minoon*, 23:1-2).

In looking closely at the second *ayah*, you will notice that the same description of the believers that is used here is also used at the end of *ayah* 45 of *Al-Baqarah*, as quoted in Chapter 5 ("Getting Spiritually Hydrated"), where Allah gives us His merciful, wise instruction on how to seek help with regards to any problem or struggle we are facing:

وَٱسْتَعِينُوا۟ بِٱلصَّبْرِ وَٱلصَّلَوٰةِ ۚ وَإِنَّهَا لَكَبِيرَةٌ إِلَّا عَلَى ٱلْخَٰشِعِينَ ﴿٤٥﴾

In this divine instruction, our Merciful Rabb is saying what has been translated to mean,

**"And seek help in *Sabr* (patiently persevering upon what nourishes the soul) and the Salaah, and truly, it is extremely heavy and hard except for the *Khaashi'oon* (the humbly and sincerely submissive)"**
(*Al-Baqarah*, 2:45).

In the second *ayah* of *Al-Mu'minoon*, the believers who have attained success are being described as *khaashi'oon*, those who are humble, sincere, and fully submissive in their Salaah. In the forty-fifth *ayah* of *Al-Baqarah*, those who are exempted from feelings of extreme overwhelm and burdensome difficulty while seeking help with *sabr* and Salaah are also described as *khaashi'oon*.

So, we can see that in both attaining success itself and in overcoming the internal weightiness of emotional and spiritual overwhelm, sincerely and humbly offering our Salaah is the answer. Thus, if we sincerely desire success in this world and in the Hereafter, we will not only establish the Salaah each day, but we will also strive to inculcate feelings of humility and submissiveness in our hearts during this spiritual routine.

*But how?* we might wonder. *Where do I even begin to fix my heart?* The answer to how we seek help in this is in *ayah* 45

itself: Begin with *sabr*, and strive to make this patient perseverance a lifestyle.

If we need further help in this, we can reflect on the next *ayah* (46), which gives us insight into how, after *sabr* and Salaah, a simple mindset shift can help us become amongst the *khaashi'oon*: Make it part of your daily lifestyle to reflect deeply on meeting Allah in the Hereafter, as this mindset is the defining trait of the *khaashi'oon*:

ٱلَّذِينَ يَظُنُّونَ أَنَّهُم مُّلَـٰقُوا۟ رَبِّهِمْ وَأَنَّهُمْ إِلَيْهِ رَٰجِعُونَ ﴿٤٦﴾

**"[The *khaashi'oon* are those] who are certain that they will meet their Rabb and that they will return to Him"** (*Al-Baqarah*, 2:46).

## Sabr As a Lifestyle

Naturally, our hearts could never attain the spiritual *rahmah* of consistent *khushoo'* (sincerity, humility, and full submissiveness) unless we show up to Salaah every day on time without fail, no matter how emotionally, mentally, or physically exhausted we feel.

In other words, if we sincerely desire to be amongst those who are successful in this world and in the Hereafter—i.e. amongst the *khaashi'oon*—then we would commit ourselves to a lifestyle of *sabr*. In this path of *sabr*, we would commit ourselves to nourishing our hearts and souls with *at least* what they minimally need to survive—*Tawheed* and Salaah—no matter what internal or external trials we are facing. Furthermore, we would commit to withholding ourselves from doing anything that would harm our hearts and souls (such as abandoning or neglecting the Salaah), no matter how tempting it might be to "just give up" or be neglectful at times.

This is the path of success, and this path of success is walked only by the sincere believer. Once we commit ourselves to striving upon this path, we begin to taste the benefits of both worldly and spiritual success, as well as perpetual protection from any significant harm—even in this world—no matter what blessing we are enjoying or painful trial we are facing.

## The Sweetness of Perpetual Success

The promise of perpetual protection from significant harm is what is being referred to in this famous prophetic hadith, in which the Messenger of Allah ﷺ said: "Amazing is the affair of the believer. Verily, every affair of his is good, and this is for no one except the believer. If something of good [or happiness] befalls him, he is grateful, and that is good for him. If something of harm befalls him, he is patient, and that is good for him" (Sahih Muslim).

When we realize that establishing the Salaah is the very essence of tasting the sweetness of this perpetual success, then we would rush to answer the call, "Come to Salaah. Come to success." Then, in answering this call while striving for *khushoo'* each day, we cannot help but feel the same calm reassurance and tranquil certainty about our own uncertain futures that my mother felt about her children's. Then we can place our trust in the divine plan of our Merciful Creator and tell our restless, distressed hearts, *You're going to be all right.*

# Soul Reflections

*As it relates to the blessing of Salaah that you just read about, write freely from your heart. Or respond to this journal prompt: Think about the blessings and success in your life that you are enjoying now or hoping to receive. What are some ways that Salaah has brought (or can bring) you or your loved ones both worldly and spiritual success? Also, have you ever allowed pursuit of worldly success to distract you from Salaah? How so?*

# Blessing 3
## *Salaah Gives Us Life*

In the previous chapter, we discussed how when we are called to prayer in the *adhaan*, we are being called to success. In the Qur'an, the last divine revelation that is a call to spiritual guidance to all of humankind until the Day of Judgment, we are over and over again called to the Salaah itself.

In the second Surah of the Qur'an, Allah says,

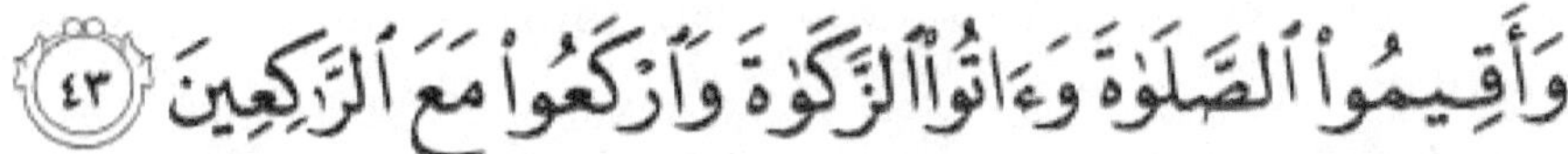

This *ayah* has been translated to mean, **"And establish the Salaah and give *zakat* and bow with those who bow [in worship and obedience]"** (*Al-Baqarah*, 2:43).

In the eleventh Surah of the Qur'an, Allah says,

وَأَقِمِ ٱلصَّلَوٰةَ طَرَفِيِ ٱلنَّهَارِ وَزُلَفًا مِّنَ ٱلَّيْلِ إِنَّ ٱلْحَسَنَٰتِ يُذْهِبْنَ ٱلسَّيِّئَاتِ ذَٰلِكَ ذِكْرَىٰ لِلذَّٰكِرِينَ

This *ayah* has been translated to mean,

**"And establish the Salaah at the two ends of the day and at the approach of the night. Indeed, good deeds do away with misdeeds. That is a reminder for those who remember"**
(*Hud*, 11:114).

In the twentieth Surah of Qur'an, Allah says,

$$\text{إِنَّنِىٓ أَنَا ٱللَّهُ لَآ إِلَٰهَ إِلَّآ أَنَا۠ فَٱعْبُدْنِى وَأَقِمِ ٱلصَّلَوٰةَ لِذِكْرِىٓ ﴿١٤﴾}$$

This *ayah* has been translated to mean,

**"Indeed, I am Allah. There is no deity except Me [i.e. nothing has the right to be worshipped except Me], so worship Me and establish the Salaah for My remembrance"**
(*Ta Ha*, 20:14).

There are numerous other *ayaat* in the Qur'an that call us to establish the Salaah. Furthermore, we see a similar pattern in the prophetic Sunnah, wherein Prophet Muhammad ﷺ repeatedly calls the believers to the foundational prayers while giving them specific instructions on how to respond to that call.

For example, in one well-known prophetic hadith, he said, "Pray as you have seen me praying. When the time of prayer arrives, let one of you announce the call to prayer for you and then let the older of you lead the prayer" (Bukhari and Muslim).

## A Merciful Call to Life

When we see these repeated calls to Salaah in the *Kitaab* and *Hikmah*, it is not without reason. As aforementioned, every part of our *deen* reflects the essence of the *rahmah* that is at the heart of our faith, and the blessings from this *rahmah* are immeasurable in human comprehension.

In His infinite knowledge, mercy, and wisdom, Allah, Ar-Rahmaan (the Most Merciful), gives us a glimpse of these immeasurable blessings when He says,

يَـٰٓأَيُّهَا ٱلَّذِينَ ءَامَنُوا۟ ٱسْتَجِيبُوا۟ لِلَّهِ وَلِلرَّسُولِ إِذَا دَعَاكُمْ لِمَا يُحْيِيكُمْ ۖ وَٱعْلَمُوٓا۟ أَنَّ ٱللَّهَ يَحُولُ بَيْنَ ٱلْمَرْءِ وَقَلْبِهِۦ وَأَنَّهُۥٓ إِلَيْهِ تُحْشَرُونَ ﴿٢٤﴾

This *ayah* has been translated to mean,

**"O you who have believed, respond to Allah and to the
Messenger when he calls you to that which
gives you life. And know that Allah intervenes
between a man and his heart and that
to Him you will be gathered"**
(*Al-Anfaal*, 8:24).

In this, we learn that when we are being called to Salaah,
we are not only being called to success, but also to that which
gives us life itself.

In another part of the Qur'an, Allah gives the description
of the believers who respond to this call to life, and the first
characteristic He mentions is their establishing of the Salaah.
Allah says,

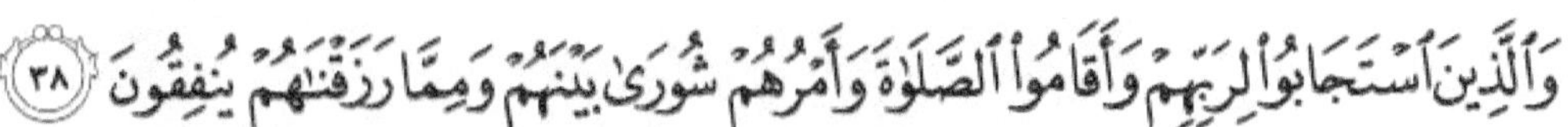

This *ayah* has been translated to mean,

**"And those who answer the Call of their Lord and
establish the Salaah, and who [conduct] their affairs
by mutual consultation, and who spend of what
We have bestowed on them"**
(*Ash-Shooraa*, 42:38).

In reflecting on this call to life, we can appreciate more
deeply how Salaah is the most essential way to hydrate our
spiritual life-veins. These *ayaat*, especially *ayah* 24 of *Al-Anfaal*, further put into perspective the analogy of just how

water is an essential source of life to the physical body, Salaah is an essential source of life to the spiritual soul. In these divine verses, we can see clearly that this analogy is not mere conjecture. It reflects the actual reality of our spiritual existence in this world, as Salaah gives us spiritual life, literally.

## Soul Reflections

*As it relates to the blessing of Salaah that you just read about, write freely from your heart. Or respond to this journal prompt: Think about a time that you felt distressed or confused and you began praying to your Merciful Rabb to grant you relief. In what ways did du'aa and Salaah "give you life" during this time?*

# Blessing 4
## *Salaah Is a Source of Divine Intervention*

In a moving Qudsi hadith, we learn about how our Merciful Creator interacts with us as we stand in Salaah, specifically during our recitation of *Al-Faatihah*, the opening Surah of Qur'an.

Prophet Muhammad ﷺ said, "Allah (Mighty and Sublime be He) said: 'I have divided the Salaah between Myself and My servant into two halves, and My servant shall have what he has asked for. When the servant says:

ٱلْحَمْدُ لِلَّهِ رَبِّ ٱلْعَـٰلَمِينَ ۝

*All praise is due to Allah, Lord of the worlds*, Allah (Mighty and Sublime be He) says: 'My servant has praised Me.' And when he says:

ٱلرَّحْمَـٰنِ ٱلرَّحِيمِ ۝

*Most Gracious, Most Merciful*, Allah (Mighty and Sublime be He) says: 'My servant has extolled Me,' and when he says:

مَـٰلِكِ يَوْمِ ٱلدِّينِ ۝

*Master of the Day of Judgment*, Allah says: 'My servant has glorified Me,' [and on one occasion He said: 'My servant has submitted to My power.'] And when he says:

إِيَّاكَ نَعْبُدُ وَإِيَّاكَ نَسْتَعِينُ ۝

*You (alone) we worship, and You (alone) we ask for help*, He says: 'This is between Me and My servant, and My servant shall have what he has asked for.' And when he says:

اهْدِنَا ٱلصِّرَٰطَ ٱلْمُسْتَقِيمَ ۝

صِرَٰطَ ٱلَّذِينَ أَنْعَمْتَ عَلَيْهِمْ غَيْرِ ٱلْمَغْضُوبِ عَلَيْهِمْ وَلَا ٱلضَّآلِّينَ ۝

*Guide us upon the Straight Path, the path of those upon whom You have bestowed Your favor, not [the path] of those who earned Your Anger, nor of those who have gone astray,* He says: 'This is for My servant, and My servant shall have what he has asked for.'" (Muslim, Malik, at-Tirmidhi, Abu-Dawud, an-Nasa'i and Ibn Majah).

## Allah Intervenes Between You and Your Heart

In the previous chapter entitled "Salah Gives Us Life," we discussed the *ayah* in which Allah says:

يَٰٓأَيُّهَا ٱلَّذِينَ ءَامَنُوا۟ ٱسْتَجِيبُوا۟ لِلَّهِ وَلِلرَّسُولِ إِذَا دَعَاكُمْ لِمَا يُحْيِيكُمْ وَٱعْلَمُوٓا۟ أَنَّ ٱللَّهَ يَحُولُ بَيْنَ ٱلْمَرْءِ وَقَلْبِهِۦ وَأَنَّهُۥٓ إِلَيْهِ تُحْشَرُونَ ۝

**"O you who have believed, respond to Allah and to the Messenger when he calls you to that which gives you life. And know that Allah intervenes between a man and his heart and that to Him you will be gathered"**
(*Al-Anfaal*, 8:24).

If we delve deeper into the meaning of this *ayah* as it relates to our spiritual lives, we find another glimpse into the immeasurable *rahmah* of our *deen*. Here, Allah is addressing one of the greatest causes of concern to the struggling soul on the brink of spiritual dehydration:

Sometimes our hearts feel so overwhelmed and distressed that we simply do not taste the sweetness of *emaan* during Salaah or other acts of worship. In fact, when we are struggling through spiritual dehydration, our hearts often feel empty, dead, or overburdened while we are praying or worshipping Allah.

Yet in this *ayah*, Allah not only reminds us to respond when we are called to that which gives us life, He also lets us know that He himself is able to intervene between us and our hurting hearts. And ultimately, it is our hurting hearts that are preventing us from feeling motivated to respond to this merciful call to life.

In this, we are reminded that by answering this call to life—even when we feel spiritually overwhelmed, empty, or demotivated—we are opening ourselves up to experiencing the deeper *rahmah* of divine intervention. This is where our Merciful Creator not only protects us from ourselves, but He also cleanses our heart from anything that is weighing heavily on it—or inclining us to spiritual dehydration and disconnecting us from Allah Himself.

However, we do not experience this divine intervention unless we show up when we are called to worship and obedience, irrespective of how we feel deep inside at the time. This divine mercy of intervention between us and our own hearts is what is being referenced in this personal reflection from my journal, which I shared earlier and wrote during a time when I myself was suffering from spiritual dehydration:

> *Struggling in your emaan? Do you feel dead inside when you pray, make du'aa, or read Qur'an?*
> *Remember this: It's okay to show up empty.*

*Just be sure to show up.*
*And your Lord will fill your heart with the spiritual fuel it*
*needs, eventually.*
*But you have to show up.*
*Show up to prayer.*
*Show up to du'aa.*
*Show up to Qur'an.*
*Just the act of showing up is a powerful act of faith.*
*Allah will take care of the rest.*

## Soul Reflections

*As it relates to the blessing of Salaah that you just read about, write freely from your heart. Or respond to this journal prompt: Think of a time that you were about to do something that you would have regretted or that would have brought harm to you, your life, or someone else in some way, yet you were blocked or prevented from it. What happened? How did Allah intervene between you and your heart?*

# Blessing 5
## *Salaah Gives Our Homes Radiance*

When I'm traveling on an airplane, I enjoy sitting near a window so I can look outside and marvel at the expansive magnificence of Allah's creation. I enjoy looking out at the clusters of clouds sitting like pillows and stretched sheets on the canopy of the radiant blue sky. When it's nighttime and the plane is ascending from the ground at take-off, I also enjoy looking out at the radiant moon and glowing stars scattered through the night sky that we are being lifted into.

One of my favorite moments is looking out the window late at night during landing as the plane is descending into the quiet darkness. On the expansive earth beneath are glowing lights from homes and streetlamps below, though most homes and streets are dark and still. Sometimes the scattered lights reflect on ponds, rivers, or lakes, giving the dark expanse an illumination like no other.

I think on these moving moments from my travels as I reflect on the prophetic hadith in which our beloved Mother Ayesha (may Allah be pleased with her) narrated that Prophet Muhammad (peace and blessings be upon him) said, "Perform a portion of your prayer in your homes, and do not make your homes as graves unlike the Jews and the Christians who placed graves in their homes. Indeed, the house in which the Qur'an is recited will be made apparent to the people of the Heaven just as the stars are made apparent to the people of the earth" (*Silsilah Ahadeeth As-Saheehah* vol. 7, Hadith n. 3112, p. 306-307, Sahih).

## The Radiance Emanates from Within

When we are granted the divine gift of a home radiating on the expanse of the earth like the stars radiate to us in the heavens, this blessed illumination is not limited to our physical home. It emanates from our bodily home as well.

In fact, it is the sincere heart in our body, which people of the world often call our "temple", that is the source of any true *noor*, any spiritual light of faith, in this world. Thus, any radiance that is gifted to our physical homes is ultimately emanating from our physical bodies, which house our hearts and souls.

When we pray and recite Qur'an, the *noor* of *emaan* emanates from within us. For this reason, true believers do not only have *noor* glowing from their houses in this world, they also have *noor* glowing from their faces as well. This spiritual light that glows from our faces due to our praying and reciting Qur'an is called the "mark of *sujood*", as discussed in this excerpt of a longer *ayah* in the Qur'an:

مُّحَمَّدٌ رَّسُولُ ٱللَّهِ وَٱلَّذِينَ مَعَهُۥٓ أَشِدَّآءُ عَلَى ٱلْكُفَّارِ رُحَمَآءُ بَيْنَهُمْ تَرَىٰهُمْ رُكَّعًا سُجَّدًا يَبْتَغُونَ فَضْلًا مِّنَ ٱللَّهِ وَرِضْوَٰنًا سِيمَاهُمْ فِى وُجُوهِهِم مِّنْ أَثَرِ ٱلسُّجُودِ ذَٰلِكَ مَثَلُهُمْ فِى ٱلتَّوْرَىٰةِ

**"Muhammad is the Messenger of Allah; and those with him are firm against the disbelievers, merciful among themselves. You see them bowing and prostrating [in Salaah], seeking bounty from Allah and [His] pleasure. Their mark is on their faces from the trace of prostration (i.e. mark of *sujood*). That is their description in the Torah..."**
(*Al-Fath*, 48:29).

In a famous prophetic hadith, Nu`am Al-Mujmir said, "Once I went up the roof of the mosque along with Abu Huraira. He performed ablution and said, 'I heard the Prophet (peace and blessings be upon him) saying, 'On the Day of Resurrection, my followers will be called *Al-Ghurr-ul-Muhajjalun* (those of magnificent, radiant beauty) from the trace of *wudhoo'*, so whoever can increase the area of his radiance should do so (i.e. by performing *wudhoo'* regularly)'" (Sahih Bukhari).

This is no doubt largely due to the divine *rahmah* of Salaah itself being a light for us. In another famous prophetic hadith, we are taught: "Purity is half of faith, and the praise of Allah fills the scale. Glorification and praise fill up what is between the heavens and the earth. Prayer is a light, charity is proof, and patience is illumination. The Quran is a proof for you or against you. All people go out early in the morning and sell themselves, either setting themselves free or ruining themselves" (Sahih Muslim).

## Soul Reflections

*As it relates to the blessing of Salaah that you just read about, write freely from your heart. Or respond to this journal prompt: Think of a surah, ayah or part of the Qur'an that is beloved to you or your family and is recited often in your home (even if only Al-Faatihah). Picture your home radiating to those in the heavens as you or your family recite it. Then reflect on why this part of the Qur'an is personally meaningful to you and/or your loved ones.*

# Blessing 6
## *Salaah Protects Us From Sin and Harm*

It is a fact of life that none of us is without fault or sin, and that none of us can escape the painful trials of this *dunya*. In a well-known prophetic hadith, we are taught: "All of the children of Adam sin, and the best of those who sin are those who constantly repent" (*Sunan al-Tirmidhi* 2499, *Sahih* by Al-Suyuti).

In the Qur'an, Allah says,

أَحَسِبَ ٱلنَّاسُ أَن يُتْرَكُوٓا۟ أَن يَقُولُوٓا۟ ءَامَنَّا وَهُمْ لَا يُفْتَنُونَ ﴿٢﴾

**"Do the people think that they will be left to say, 'We believe' and they will not be put to trial?"**
(*Al-'Ankaboot*, 29:2).

So, one might ask, *If we are going to fall into sin and difficulty no matter what we do, what exactly is Salaah protecting us from?* In a sentence: Salaah is protecting us from sin corrupting our hearts and destroying our lives, and it is protecting our souls from misery and failing our worldly trials.

Spiritually, the harm of being corrupted by sin is immeasurable by human estimation. In the following entry from my personal journal, I caution my own struggling heart, as well as my sisters and brothers in faith:

*Beware, though we all sin and are in need of Allah's mercy, sin should not be taken lightly. Sin is destructive to your life and soul, and it is destructive to your character and sanity.*

*Sin without repentance is like terminal illness without treatment. In the early stages, the disease of sin (like the disease of the body) is barely detectable. But as it progresses, it obstructs the very life veins of spiritual life.*

*By Allah, a person cannot indulge in open, unrepentant sin except that he or she falls seriously ill, spiritually and mentally. And every part of the body bears testimony to the ailing of the spirit.*

*The tongue becomes diseased and speaks lies as truth. The eyes become blurred and see darkness as light. The hands reach frantically for that which would wreak only more havoc to the spirit—and the limbs fall in submission. The mind caves in illness, convinced that evil is good. And the heart becomes hardened and rusted, until it cries out in conviction to its life of sin, "Ah! You are my lord, and I am your servant!"*

So, when we learn that Salaah protects us from sin and harm, this divine mercy is not in reference to being protected from the human experience, as we will all fall into sin at times and be tested in this world. Rather, it is in reference to Salaah protecting us from the human catastrophe of sin destroying our hearts, minds, and lives.

In the Qur'an, Allah instructs us:

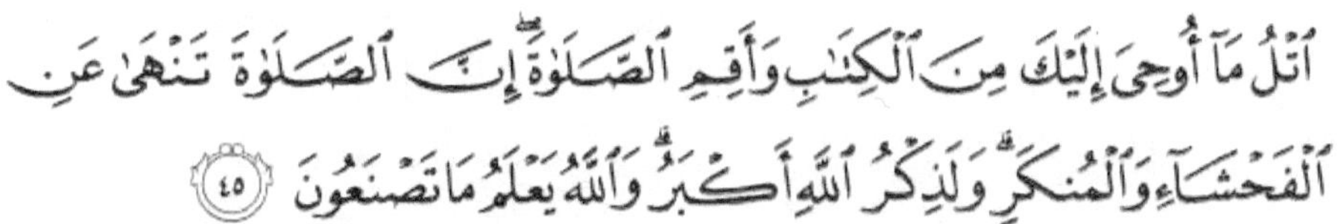

**"Recite what has been revealed to you of the Book, and establish the Salaah. Indeed, the Salaah keeps one from the great sins and evil deeds. And the remembrance of Allah is greater. And Allah knows that which you do"**
*(Al-'Ankaboot, 29:45).*

# Soul Reflections

*As it relates to the blessing of Salaah that you just read about, write freely from your heart. Or respond to this journal prompt: Think of a sin or fault that inspires in you regret or shame, yet you struggle to resist it. Or think of some harm or trial that you fear deeply in this world. Reflect on how you plan to increase your Salaah (i.e. spending more time in sajdah, praying Qiyaam regularly, etc.) as a means to better protect yourself from this sin or from the harm you fear. What du'aa will you make in sujood, Qunoot, or after you pray?*

# Blessing 7
## *Salaah Erases Sins*

In addition to protecting us from falling into great sin and harm, Salaah is a means through which the sins that we do fall into are erased from our record completely. In this way, our Book of Deeds can reflect that we never committed the sin at all.

The famous Companion Abu Hurayrah reported that the Messenger of Allah (peace and blessings be upon him) once asked: "What do you think if there was a river by the door of any one of you and he bathed in it five times a day, would there be any trace of dirt left on him?" They said, "No trace of dirt would be left on him." He said, "That is like the five daily prayers, by means of which Allah erases sin" (Bukhari and Muslim).

Even for those sins that remain written in our record, Salaah grants us the opportunity to be forgiven for them. As a result, any due punishment that we deserve as a result is erased from our fate.

In the Qur'an, Allah says,

$$\text{وَٱلَّذِينَ إِذَا فَعَلُوا۟ فَٰحِشَةً أَوْ ظَلَمُوٓا۟ أَنفُسَهُمْ ذَكَرُوا۟ ٱللَّهَ فَٱسْتَغْفَرُوا۟ لِذُنُوبِهِمْ وَمَن يَغْفِرُ ٱلذُّنُوبَ إِلَّا ٱللَّهُ وَلَمْ يُصِرُّوا۟ عَلَىٰ مَا فَعَلُوا۟ وَهُمْ يَعْلَمُونَ ﴿١٣٥﴾}$$

**"And those who, when they have committed *faahishah* (fornication, adultery, sexual lewdness, immorality, etc.) or wronged themselves with evil, remember Allah and ask forgiveness for their sins - and none can**

**forgive sins but Allah - And do not persist in what [wrong] they have done, while they know"**
*(Aali 'Imraan, 3:135).*

It is this *ayah* being referenced in the prophetic hadith in which Abu Bakr al-Siddeeq reported: "I heard the Messenger of Allah (peace and blessings of Allah be upon him) say: 'There is no one who commits a sin then purifies himself well and stands and prays two *rak'ah*'s [of voluntary Salaah], then asks Allah for forgiveness, but Allah will forgive him.' Then he recited this verse: 'And those who, when they have committed *faahishah* (illegal sexual acts) or wronged themselves with evil, remember Allah and ask forgiveness for their sins — and none can forgive sins but Allah — and do not persist in what [wrong] they have done, while they know' (3:135)." (Abu Dawood 1521, Sahih by al-Albaani).

It is interesting to note that in the Qur'an, the term *faahishah* refers not only to fornication and adultery but also to any sexual lewdness or immorality, including homosexual acts. Thus, we get a further glimpse into the immeasurable mercy of Allah that we are gifted through the Salaah, as it is a means of being forgiven for even major sins, particularly when we are sincere in striving against our *nafs* and seeking forgiveness for any number of carnal temptations that we fall into in this world—even when we struggle with sin repeatedly.

The famous Companion Anas (may Allah be pleased with him) said, "I heard the Messenger of Allah (peace and blessings of Allah be upon him) say: 'Allah the Almighty said, "O son of Adam, so long as you call upon Me and ask of Me, I shall forgive you for what you have done, and I shall not mind. O son of Adam, were your sins to reach the clouds of the sky and were you then to ask forgiveness of Me, I would forgive you. O son of Adam, were you to come to Me with sins nearly as great as the earth and were you then to face Me, ascribing no partner to Me, I would bring you forgiveness nearly as great as it" (at-Tirmidhi and Ahmad ibn Hanbal).

Moreover, in the Qur'an, our Merciful Rabb lets us know that there is no limit to the amount or type of sins that He is willing to forgive:

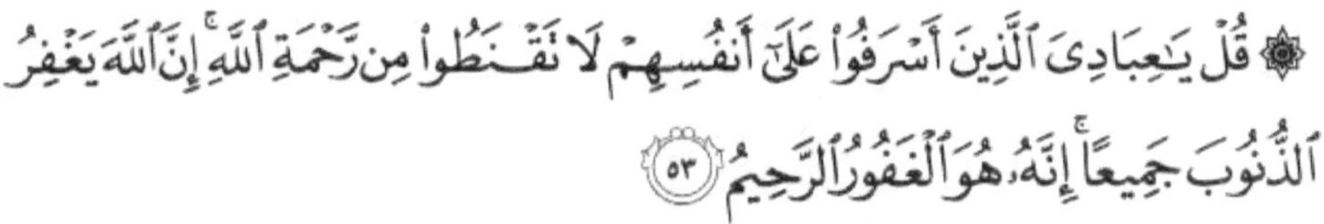

**"Say, O My slaves who have wronged their souls! Despair not of the mercy of Allah. Verily, Allah forgives all sins. Truly, He is Oft-Forgiving, Most Merciful"**
(*Az-Zumar*, 39:53).

And yes, this immeasurable mercy and forgiveness extends to even the sin of *shirk*, so long as the person does not die upon it—i.e. so long as they repent before their soul is taken.

# Soul Reflections

*As it relates to the blessing of Salaah that you just read about, write freely from your heart. Or respond to this journal prompt: Think of a sin that you desperately hope to be forgiven for or to have erased from your record. Does your commitment to Salaah reflect your sincere desire for forgiveness and pardon? If not, why not? What do you think is preventing you from utilizing Salaah as a means to forgiveness and pardon? And how are you committed to changing or improving your relationship with Salaah today, moving forward?*

# Blessing 8
## Salaah Is Wealth for Our Souls

One Friday as I read and reflected on the *ayaat* of *Surah Al-Kahf*, I wrote this personal reminder in my journal and then shared it with my sisters and brothers in faith: *Read Al-Kahf. Make du'aa. Send prayers of peace and blessings upon Prophet Muhammad (sallallaahu'alayhi wa sallam). And pray Salaah on time with khushoo' (sincere humility and reflection) today and every day thereafter.*

*Our souls sometimes need the shelter of a spiritual cave to refocus and remind the heart what's most important in life.*

*So, pray.*

*Pray for your heart.*

*Pray for your life.*

*Pray for your soul.*

*And pray for wealth in abundance. But do not seek to adorn a graveyard. For there is no benefit in piling up on wealth and possessions when they are only intended for the dead.*

*When we ask Allah for worldly abundance and success while neglecting our spiritual health, we are like the one investing all of their wealth into adorning a grave. Dead bodies cannot benefit from the joys of life—and dead hearts cannot benefit from the blessings of life.*

*So yes, pray for wealth. But ask the Creator to help your heart understand that the greatest wealth is not found in material possessions, but in your nearness to Him.*

**Salaah Is Your Wealth**

The famous Companion Abu Dharr (may Allah be pleased with him) reported, "Some of the people from among the

Companions of the Apostle of Allah (may peace be upon him) said to him, 'O Messenger of Allah, the rich have taken away [all the] reward. They observe Salaah as we do; they keep the fasts as we keep, and they give *sadaqah* out of their surplus riches.' Upon this he (the Holy Prophet) said: 'Has Allah not prescribed for you [a course] by following which you can [also] do *sadaqah*? In every declaration of the glorification of Allah (i.e. saying *SubhaanAllah*) there is a *sadaqah*, and every *takbir* (i.e. saying *Allahu'akbar*) is *sadaqah*, and every praise of His (saying *Alhamdulillah*) is *sadaqah* and every declaration that He is One (*Laa ilaaha illaAllah*) is *sadaqah*...'' (Sahih Muslim, Book 5, No. 2198).

And we find this wealth of *sadaqah* in every *dhikr*, movement, and *raka'ah* of the Salaah.

Moreover, Prophet Muhammad (peace and blessings be upon him) taught us that the Salaah is like a savings account for the wealth of good deeds we amass in this world. He said: ''The first matter that the slave [of Allah] will be brought to account for on the Day of Judgment is the Salaah. If it is sound, then the rest of his deeds will be sound. And if it is corrupt, then the rest of his deeds will be corrupt'' (al-Tabarani, *Sahih al-Jami*).

In this, we learn that the Salaah is the means through which any good we do in this world is counted as part of our spiritual wealth in the Hereafter. Therefore, we should view the immeasurable blessing of Salaah as our primary means of attaining any lasting wealth in this world.

## Cherish Every Moment of Salaah

Given that Salaah is the foundation of any lasting wealth in this world, we should cherish every movement and *dhikr* we recite in our formal prayer. In this, we should not rush through the sacred moments that we are blessed to spend with our Merciful Rabb, and we should not allow our minds to wander aimlessly. I remind my own restless heart of the sacredness of Salaah in my journal:

*This.*

*Resting your forehead on the ground.*

*Wetting your arms and face with the water of wudhoo'.*

*Raising your hands in supplication to the Almighty.*

*Tears streaming down your cheeks as you beg His forgiveness.*

*This.*

*It's the only reason you are alive.*

*It's the only reason you have a place on earth.*

*It's the only reason you have air in your lungs, a tongue in your mouth, and the blessings you enjoy each day.*

*So dear soul, why do you rush through these spiritual moments, mind wandering, heart disengaged—as if you've something more urgent, more important to do?*

*Are you in a hurry to gather yet more of those things that you'll be compelled to leave behind when you are lowered beneath the ground?*

## Soul Reflections

*As it relates to the blessing of Salaah that you just read about, write freely from your heart. Or respond to this journal prompt: What goals of building material wealth or attaining worldly success do you have for yourself and your family in this world? What are you doing to attain these goals and to hold yourself and your loved ones accountable? How can you use this same mindset and approach to build and secure spiritual wealth for yourself and your family through the obligatory and voluntary Salaah, like Qiyaam?*

# Blessing 9
## *Salaah Offers Us Help and Health*

When we are struggling with anything and need help, Salaah itself is a source of help—even when we need help in maintaining the Salaah itself. In the Qur'an, Allah says:

**"And seek help through *sabr* and Salaah, and indeed, it is difficult except for the *khaashi'oon* (those who are humbly submissive to Allah)"**
(*Al-Baqarah*, 2:45).

Though this *ayah* was discussed earlier, it is beneficial to our struggling hearts to be again reminded of the weighty message and immeasurable *rahmah* being conveyed in it.

Whatever we are struggling with and being tested with in this world, whether personal or spiritual, we will find our greatest source of help through *sabr*—patiently persevering upon what will nourish our souls and better our lives, even when we feel overwhelmed, burdened, and unmotivated—and the Salaah.

## Salaah Improves Our Physical Health

Moreover, the source of help and divine mercy that Salaah offers us in this world has tangible evidence, even in our physical health.

For example, a study about the Muslim prayer that is recorded in *The Journal of Physical Therapy Science* and published in the *US National Library of Medicine* via The National Center for Biotechnology Information reports:

"The results of the present study show that the dynamic stability of the subjects practicing Islamic prayer was significantly better than that of the non-practicing individuals. The results could be related to the physical and mental activities associated with Islamic prayer. Religious meditation and prayers have been found to promote relaxation and a healthier, more balanced condition of the human mind and body. Studies on the benefits of 'salat' have revealed that it improves not only spiritual well-being, but also mental and physical health, improving muscle strength, joint mobility and blood circulation, when performed correctly and with the right postures" (2013).

There are many other similar studies confirming these physical health benefits of the Salaah and more.

## Soul Reflections

*As it relates to the blessing of Salaah that you just read about, write freely from your heart. Or respond to this journal prompt: What are some goals or trials that you need (or would like) help with in this world? Are you seeking help from worldly resources or other people? If so, how so? In what ways can you become more mindful about also using the tools of sabr and Salaah while seeking help in these?*

# Blessing 10
## *It's Okay To Be Imperfect*

In closing, it is beneficial to remind our struggling hearts that just as there is no perfect person in this world, there is no perfect Salaah performed by any fallible human being in this world. And that's okay. The blessings of the Salaah are still for us, despite our inevitable imperfections as struggling souls in this *dunya*.

In one prophetic hadith, Prophet Muhammad (peace and blessings be upon him) describes how much of the Salaah is actually recorded for us in this world, and the most that he mentions being credited for anyone is one half.

The famous Companion 'Ammaar ibn Yaasir (may Allah be pleased with him) said, "I heard the Messenger of Allah (peace and blessings of Allah be upon him) say: 'A person may offer a prayer and nothing of it is recorded for him except one tenth of it, one ninth of it, one eighth of it, one seventh of it, one sixth of it, one fifth of it, one quarter of it, one third of it, or half of it' (Ahmad 18415, *Hasan* by al-Albaani in *Saheeh al-Jaami*ʿ 1626).

Here, it is helpful to remind ourselves that Allah Himself is fully aware of our human faults and struggles, even those that make the Salaah itself heavy and burdensome to our imperfect hearts at times. In fact, as discussed earlier, this human imperfection is precisely the message that He is conveying to us after He lets us know that the Salaah will help us get through whatever we are going through right now:

وَٱسۡتَعِينُوا۟ بِٱلصَّبۡرِ وَٱلصَّلَوٰةِ وَإِنَّهَا لَكَبِيرَةٌ إِلَّا عَلَى ٱلۡخَٰشِعِينَ ٤٥

**"And seek help through *sabr* and Salaah, and indeed,
it is difficult [and heavy] except for the *khaashi'oon*
(the humbly submissive)"**
(*Al-Baqarah*, 2:45).

In this merciful reminder, our Compassionate, Loving Rabb is assuring us that He knows very well how much our struggling hearts feel heavy and burdened on the path of *sabr* and Salaah. Yet He reassures us that our patient perseverance and maintaining of the prayer remain our source of help on the very path that we are struggling on at this time.

Here, as alluded to earlier, it is relevant to note that an inherent part of *sabr* is accepting that we are imperfect and will thus fall short and sin at times. Nevertheless, our success lies in never giving up on ourselves or our souls no matter how imperfect, flawed and sinful we remain in this world.

Also, we should understand that sometimes when we are facing difficulty in our Salaah, it could be due to underlying mental health issues or emotional trauma that isn't our fault. While these trials are not necessarily due to any sin or lacking *emaan* on our part, they are very real and should not be trivialized or viewed as insignificant. Nor should they be used as an excuse to neglect or abandon the Salaah altogether.

In many cases, these underlying mental health conditions and emotional wounds can be the underlying cause of what feels like spiritual dehydration itself. Thus, as we embrace Salaah as the foundation of our day and lives, it is a crucial part of our daily spiritual nourishment to be compassionate and patient with ourselves on this path, which is the very essence of living a life of *sabr* in this world.

Regardless of the underlying reason behind Salaah feeling burdensome to us, in the above *ayah*, our Merciful Rabb is assuring as that if we stay the course of *sabr* and Salaah and remain humbly submissive, He will lift the difficulty and weightiness from our hearts.

However, just as is the case with sin itself, this lifting of the burden will not necessarily remove from us our humanity or completely erase from our lives any worldly trials or underlying mental health conditions or any lingering effects of emotional trauma. But it will certainly allow us to be relieved from any unnecessary or additional burdens that we would carry if neglect or abandon our Salaah.

When we embrace the path of seeking help through *sabr* and Salaah each day, it is quite possible that the Salaah will become for us—in our own "perfectly imperfect" way—as it was for the beloved Prophet and Messenger of Allah (peace and blessings be upon him): the greatest source of joy and a "coolness of the eye" for us in this world.

As dear struggling soul, as you take this path, know that a great blessed bounty awaits you from your Lord. Not because you were perfect, but because you held onto your faith and Salaah, and thus were counted amongst the believers in this world despite your flaws and imperfections.

Allah says:

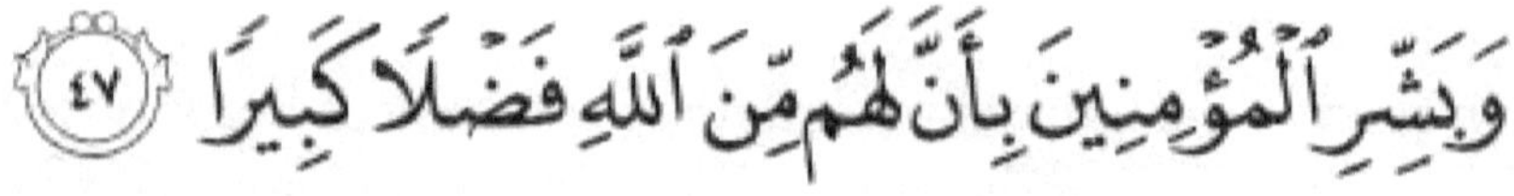

**"And give good tidings to the believers that they will
have from Allah great bounty"**
(*Al-Ahzaab*, 33:47).

# Soul Reflections

*As it relates to the blessing of Salaah that you just read about, write freely from your heart. Or share your honest personal reflections to this excerpt from the journal of Umm Zakiyyah: "It's true that many people suffer in the Hereafter due to underestimating the severity of Allah's punishment, but perhaps more suffer due to underestimating the vastness of Allah's mercy. For if they only knew the mercy of Allah, they wouldn't have given themselves to a life void of Salaah and repentance."*

# Closing Notes
## *Affirmations for Compassionate Presence*

*When I feel broken, I will pray. When I feel weak, I will pray. When I feel empty, I will pray. Then I will trust that my Merciful Creator will write me down amongst His most beloved companions of Salaah, even if I myself feel undeserving of this honor.*

• • •

*I will show up for my soul, even if I show up empty, and I fully trust my Most Merciful Creator is granting me the spiritual fuel I need, even when I'm unable to perceive it.*

# Also By Umm Zakiyyah

*If I Should Speak*
*A Voice*
*Footsteps*
*Realities of Submission*
*Hearts We Lost*
*The Friendship Promise*
*Muslim Girl*
*His Other Wife*
*UZ Short Story Collection*
*The Test Paper* (a children's book)
*Pain. From the Journal of Umm Zakiyyah*
*Broken yet Faithful. From the Journal of Umm Zakiyyah*
*Faith. From the Journal of Umm Zakiyyah*
*Let's Talk About Sex and Muslim Love*
*Reverencing the Wombs That Broke You: A Daughter of Rape and Abuse Inspires Healing and Healthy Family*
*Prejudice Bones in My Body: Essays on Muslim Racism, Bigotry and Spiritual Abuse*
*And Then I Gave Up: Essays About Faith and Spiritual Crisis in Islam*
*I Almost Left Islam: How I Reclaimed My Faith*
*The Abuse of Forgiveness: Manipulation and Harm in the Name of Emotional Healing*
*even if. bits and pieces from the heart of Umm Zakiyyah*
*No One Taught Me the Human Side of Islam: The Muslim Hippie's Story of Living with Bipolar Disorder*
*He Asked About Islam*
*Alone, But In the Company of Your Lord*
*Come Back To Allah, Dear Soul: Salaah Coursebook*
*Dear Soul, It's Time: A Journey of Coming Back To Allah*
*I'm Divorced Now: Heartbreak and Healing*
*What Did You Expect? Lessons on Spiritual Honesty*
*Dear Struggling Soul: Affirmations for Spiritual Self-Compassion*
*Nurturing the Nafs: Emotional Honesty for the Female Soul*
*Learning Love: Self-Care Journal*

# Read FREE Books by Umm Zakiyyah

# About the Author

Known for her soul-touching books and spiritual reflections on the Qur'an and emotional healing, Umm Zakiyyah is a world-renowned author and soul-care mentor.

Umm Zakiyyah studied Arabic, Qur'an, Islamic sciences, *'aqeedah*, and *tafseer* in America, Egypt, and Saudi Arabia for more than fifteen years. She currently teaches *tajweed* (rules of reciting Qur'an), *tafseer* (explanation of the meaning of the Qur'an), and *tadabbur* (deep reflections on the Qur'an) via uzhearthub.com.

Daughter of American converts to Islam, Umm Zakiyyah (also known by her birth name Ruby Moore and her "Muslim" name Baiyinah Siddeeq) is the internationally acclaimed, award-winning author of more than twenty-five books, including novels, short stories, and self-help. Her books are used in high schools and universities in the United States and worldwide, and her work has been translated into multiple languages. Her work has earned praise from writers, professors, and filmmakers. Her novel *His Other Wife* is now a short film.

Dr. Robert D. Crane, advisor to former US President Nixon, said of Umm Zakiyyah, "…no amount of training can bring a person without superb, natural talent to captivate the reader as she does and exert a permanent intellectual and emotional impact."

Professor K. Bryant of Howard University said of *If I Should Speak*, "The novel belongs to…a genre worthy of scholarly study."

Umm Zakiyyah has a BA degree in Elementary Education, an MA in English Language Learning, and Cambridge's CELTA (Certificate in English Language Teaching to Adults).

In 2020, she founded an online university to share the life lessons she learned on her emotional and spiritual healing journey. For information on UZ courses, go to **uzhearthub.com** or **sqsoul.com** or **uzuniversity.com**

Read UZ Books:: **uzauthor.com**

Instagram: @uzauthor

Facebook: ummzakiyyahpage

YouTube: uzreflections

# Glossary of Common Arabic and Islamic Terms

***adab***: good manners; showing others humble respect; Islamic etiquette

***alhamdulillah***: "All praise belongs to Allah (God, the Creator) alone"

**Allah**: Arabic term for God; the only One who has the right to be worshipped

***'aqeedah***: foundational beliefs of the Islamic spiritual way of life

***ayaat***: plural form of *ayah*

***ayah:*** verse from Qur'an or divine sign

***'ayn***: (literally "eye") used in reference to "the evil eye," which is often rooted in harmful envy or unhealthy admiration of someone devoid of mentioning Allah

***bid'ah***: sinful innovation in religion

***bi'idhnillaah***: "with the help of Allah (the Creator)"

***da'wah***: teaching others about Islam; inviting others to spiritual guidance

***deen***: spiritual way of life; religion

***dhikr***: sincere mention or remembrance of Allah (the Creator)

***dhulm***: wrongdoing or oppression (of others or one's own soul)

***du'aa***: prayerful supplication; informal prayer

***dunya***: this worldly life as opposed to the Hereafter

***emaan***: sincere faith; authentic spirituality; belief in Islam; *Tawheed*

***faahishah***: immorality, usually of a sexual nature

***faasiq***: evildoer; a person living in open sin or wrongdoing

**fatwa**: Islamic ruling or opinion given by a scholar

***fisq***: evil, corruption, or clear sin and wrongdoing

***fitnah***: difficult trial

***fitrah***: inherent inborn nature of every human soul to worship Allah alone and to live a spiritually and morally upright life

***ghayb***: unseen

***gheebah***: backbiting; saying anything about a fellow Muslim that if they were to hear it, they would dislike it

***ghuroor***: spiritual self-deception

***halaal***: divinely blessed or permissible

***haraam***: divinely forbidden or sinful

***hasad***: envy that is sinful and spiritually destructive

***hasan***: good; often used in reference to the rating of "good" regarding the strength of authenticity of a prophetic hadith

***hijrah***: migration from one land to another for the sake of your faith; moving from a place that harms the soul to a place that nourishes the soul

*hikmah:* literally "wisdom"; often used in reference to the divinely inspired prophetic wisdom

*iftaar:* the moment of breaking one's fast at sunset

*ijmaa':* unanimous agreement amongst the earliest Muslims and scholars

*istighfaar:* uttering supplications seeking Allah's forgiveness

*Istikhaarah:* prayer and supplication for making a decision about something

*istislaam:* spiritual surrender

*jahiliyyah:* pre-Islamic days of spiritual and moral ignorance before the prophetic assignment was given to Prophet Muhammad (peace be upon him); any mindset or life path that mirrors this spiritual and moral ignorance

*Jahannam:* Hellfire (also called Hell)

*Jannah:* Paradise (also called Heaven)

*kaafir:* disbeliever; any person who rejects a foundational part of Islam, who knowingly rejects a well-established principle or teaching of Islam, or who knowingly introduces or accepts any teaching that forbids what Allah allows or permits what Allah has forbidden regarding any matter wherein disagreement is not permitted

*khaashi'oon:* people who are defined by their *khushoo'*; those who are sincerely and humbly submissive in their worship and obedience to Allah

*khula':* female-initiation marriage dissolution

*khushoo':* sincerity and humility of the heart and soul; deep concentration in *Salaah* such that the heart is consistently spiritually nourished by its sincere and humble connection to its Creator in every part of prayer

*kibr:* sinful pride or pride that is spiritually harmful; looking down on others and rejecting the truth

*kitaab:* literally "book"; often used in reference to the Qur'an (i.e. the Book of Allah)

*kufr:* disbelief; spiritual blasphemy; any belief, speech or action that cancels one's *emaan*

*Laa ilaaha illaa Allah:* statement of *Tawheed* or declaration of faith that means, "Nothing has the right to be worshipped except Allah alone"

*madhloom:* one who has been wronged, oppressed, or suffered from *dhulm*

*mahr:* obligatory gift given to woman upon marriage; dowry

*nafs:* inner-self or desires that are self-serving and spiritually harmful

*nameemah:* gossip or tale-carrying

*naseehah*: sincere advice offered to inspire soul-nourishment and life betterment in the one being advised

*nikaah*: Islamic marriage contract; often written and signed before the man and woman live together

*qadar*: divine decree; predestination

*qawwaam*: the man's divinely assigned role of being the maintainer, provider, and protector of women in the home and society

*Qiyaam ul-Layl*: the blessed night prayer, prayed in last third of night

*Rabb:* another name for Allah that refers to His Lordship over creation; Creator, Owner and Manager of all that exists

*rahmah*: divine mercy

*rak'ah*: one unit of *Salaah* (formal prayer)

*riba*: usury

*riyaa*: insincerity; showing off; seeking the pleasure, admiration, reward, or attention of other than Allah

*ruqyaa'*: spiritual healing that includes reciting the Qur'an over someone and/or reciting *dhikr* and prayerful supplications for the purpose of healing illness or removing the effects of *'ayn* or *sihr* on someone

*sabr*: sincere patience; patiently persevering upon that which benefits one's life and soul, and patiently persevering in abstaining from that which harms one's life and the soul

*sadaqah*: voluntary, non-obligatory charity

*sahih/saheeh*: authentic; the highest grade of a hadith's authenticity

*sajdah*: prostrating the forehead on the floor in submission to Allah

*Salaah*: the five foundational prayers: *Fajr, Dhuhr, 'Asr, Maghrib,* and *'Ishaa'*; second pillar of Islam; formal prayer, whether optional or obligatory

*sallallaahu'alayhi wa sallam*: (ﷺ) prayers of peace and blessing upon the Prophet

*shahaadah*: formal declaration of faith that marks one's entry into Islam: "I bear witness that nothing has the right to be worshipped except Allah alone, and I bear witness that Muhammad is His slave and messenger"; sincere testimony of *Tawheed* recited repeatedly throughout a Muslim's life

**Shaytaan**: the devil; Satan

*shirk*: assigning divine attributes to creation or creation's attributes to the Creator

*shukr*: sincere gratefulness, thankfulness or gratitude

*sihr*: often referred to as "black magic": when someone works with the jinn to harm someone or get a specific outcome in this world

*soorah/surah*: divine chapter of the Qur'an

***SubhaanAllah***: statement of glorification of Allah: "Glory to Allah, and Exalted and High is He above any imperfection"

***sujood***: another term for *sajdah:* prostrating the forehead on the floor in submission to Allah

**Sunnah**: prophetic guidance or example; the life and teachings of Prophet Muhammad (peace and blessings be upon him)

**Sunni**: a description of Muslims who affiliate with understanding and living Islam based on the prophetic Sunnah

***tafseer***: authentic interpretation and spiritual explanation of the *ayaat* of Qur'an

***tajweed***: rules of reciting the Qur'an based on one or more of the seven authentic prophetic recitation styles

***taqwaa***: sincere God-consciousness and daily soul care that protects the heart from corruption and the soul from spiritual harm in the Hereafter

***tawakkul***: sincere trust in the wisdom and decisions of the Creator

***tawbah***: sincere repentance; turning one's life around as a form of seeking forgiveness for past sins and wrongdoing

***Tawheed***: Oneness of Allah; singling out the Creator alone in worship; authentic monotheism; sincere belief in the Oneness of Allah

***tazkiyyatun-nafs***: purification of the soul; spiritual nourishment that is attained through sincerity while fulfilling the required and optional acts of worship in Islam

***'ulamaa***: scholars; people of spiritual knowledge (plural of *'aalim*)

***ummah***: all Muslims from every generation; worldwide faith community

***uswah***: example or pattern to be followed by others

***Witr***: highly recommended prayer performed after *Ishaa'* or at the closing of *Qiyaam ul-Layl* and consists of three units of prayer (odd number)

***wudhoo'***: ritual ablution that is done before *Salaah*

***zakaah/zakaat***: obligatory charity paid from one's wealth and given to the needy

***zina***: fornication or adultery

# REFERENCES

AlAbdulwahab, S.S., Kachanatuh, S.J., and Oluseye, K. (2013), "Physical Activity Associated with Prayer Regimes Improves Standing Dynamic Balance of Healthy People." *The Journal of Physical Therapy Science* via *US National Library of Medicine* and The National Center for Biotechnology Information. Retrieved May 5, 2021 from
https://www.ncbi.nlm.nih.gov/pmc/articles/PMC3885840/

www.ingramcontent.com/pod-product-compliance
Lightning Source LLC
Chambersburg PA
CBHW051454140726
47987CB00006B/2703